TH

MW01601613

THE AETH MYSTERY

A ROSICRUCIAN TEXT

First Edition 1914
The Philosophical Publishing Co.

New Edition 2019
Edited by Tarl Warwick

COPYRIGHT AND DISCLAIMER

The first edition of this work is in the public domain having been written prior to 1925. This edition, with its cover art and format, is all rights reserved.

In no way may this text be construed as encouraging or condoning any harmful or illegal act. In no way may this text be construed as able to diagnose, treat, cure, or prevent any disease, injury, symptom, or condition.

FOREWORD

This following booklet is an introductory and somewhat self-advertising work released long ago by the FRC- the Fraternity of the Rosy Cross, a Rosicrucian order.

The content is variable; some dense, some more straight-forward, with admonitions to consider joining the fraternity peppered throughout the booklet. Oddly, unlike many contemporary works, it contains no advertising page at the end and does not include mailing slips, only a basic mailing address.

The work covers some of the basic principles of the fraternity- namely its focus on silence, obedience to basic principles, and eager adoption of a semi-ascetic lifestyle. Some of the allusions deal with concepts which were fleshed out in further literature made available only to "advanced" members, such as the "Oriental Breast Drill"- apparently an allusion to breathing methods of a Yogic sort.

It should be noted that the company which originally released this and other similar works is still around to this day in Quakertown, having been properly incorporated in the 1920s. The road it is on is even named after the FRC's Clymer himself.

This edition of "The Aeth Mystery" has been carefully edited for format and content. Care has been taken to retain all original intent and meaning.

THE AETH MYSTERY

INTRODUCTORY

This booklet is issued only in order that it may be the means of giving information to those who are interested in what is known as the Higher Occult, or the true Mystic, in its highest and deepest form. It has nothing at all to do with those forms of the mysterious which come under the head of trickery or of fortune telling, and those other various doctrines which, though called Occult and Mystic, are the damnation of Religion, of Philosophy, of Science, and of souls themselves, because they claim to be what they are not, and because they bring reproach upon that which is, and that which is good.

Herein we indicate that which belongs to the legitimate Occult and Mystic, that which is of the Soul, and has the powers of the Soul. We give information of that Mystic Fraternity which has existed ever since history began, and which continues to exist. The Mystic Fraternity to which we refer, is based upon the fundamental truth that man is, but that, aside from his physical being, there is another being, called by us, the Soul, which, when developed, awakened, and Illuminated, is far greater in its powers than is the power possessed by either body or mind or even by body and mind combined.

We ask no one either to believe, or to have faith in, the statements made. We do not appeal to the skeptic, the materialist, nor even to the materialistic scientist. We appeal only to those who are deeply interested in the truth, and who are eager to learn. We desire to give information only to those who are truly interested in the deeper and more sublime things in life, to those who already believe in the powers of the Soul, and in the Immortality of man.

4

THE AETH MYSTERY

THE AGES OF GREATEST ENLIGHTENMENT

Let the materialist, the materialistic scientist, even the religious fanatic, ask himself this question: "In what age, or in what ages, has civilization reached its highest stage of development?" That is, in what age or ages has man been at his best? What religious faith and practice prevailed when man was at his best, at his greatest power?

When we study the history of the ages gone by, when we consider Egypt with its sublime civilization, we find that art and culture, the love of the beautiful, and the power of man was at its highest in that age in which the Mystic Priesthood was at its height, when no man could become King unless he had also become an Initiate, unless he had been trained and taught by the Priesthood of Egypt. In fact, Science, Art, Culture, Refinement, was at its very highest when Egypt was ruled by its Initiate-Kings; and the downfall of Egypt started only when the rulers of Egypt were men who had not been taught in the Priesthood of Egypt.

Not even today has mankind reached anywhere near the state of development in any one line that Egypt had reached. In the Arts we have much to say; but no man yet has solved the mystery of colors used by the ancient Egyptians. In buildings we have accomplished much; but no man yet has been able to mix the cements so that they will hold throughout the ages. And, as to architecture, we are very far from the ancients. As in these things, so in many other things; and, when we enter the domain of religion and religious practices, then we may well shed tears of pity. In that age men believed and lived; while today there is neither faith nor practice, but only words, words, which amount to nothing, and accomplish nothing, because they are not of the heart.

THE AETH MYSTERY

And, as to statecraft, no doubt we have great statesmen; but our statesmanship is not strong enough to offset the evils of selfish interest which is ruling today, and which gives nothing to mankind generally, but takes all to itself. But, in Egypt, as well as in Greece, they had a special, and a very good way, of dealing with those statesmen who betrayed the trust of the people.

In those countries, under the rule of the Initiate-Kings, the statesman that proved false to his trust, that betrayed his constituents, was punished with death. It is needless to say that this was seldom necessary. Also, in like manner, the Priesthood and the Training School for Initiates dealt with the Neophyte that proved false. It must not be understood, however, that, in the case of the Neophyte, the Priesthood either put him to death or saw that it was done. On the contrary, the Priesthood had nothing whatever to do with it. According to the Occult Law, the Neophyte, by his own thoughts and acts, metes out his own punishment. The Law of Punishment is this. In the Halls of Mystery, when the Neophyte follows certain Invocations, which lead him to Mastership, he sets into motion certain Forces; and these Forces, terrible and sublime for good, are the very Forces that react upon himself if he proves faithless to the Order and its teachings.

This every Neophyte understood at the time of entrance into the Temple as a Neophyte; and, if he proved faithless, and thus sealed his own death warrant, he had no one to blame but himself. In the mighty Fraternities, certain instructions and Sacred Mantrams are taught, which, if faithfully followed, will lead to Initiation and Soul Illumination, even to Immortality, but which, if the Neophyte proves false to his vows, will react upon himself, and end in death. It can not be otherwise. And why should it be otherwise? For every fair mind will admit that to take the solemn obligation that is taken when the Degree is conferred upon the Neophyte who has found the Light, should forever hold the Brother faithful to his most Sacred Vows, Vows which do not interfere with his liberty, but which make him one with the sublime Fraternity, and which he should always hold most sacred. And it is safe to say that he will always hold them sacred unless, through certain acts and through dabbling with things profane, he is led to degeneration and weakness of mind.

It is but fair to think, and to say, that no one entering the Temple and taking the Vow, will prove faithless unless there is, within his soul, within his make-up, a weakness that prevents him from being a man in the true sense of the word. Can we say, can we claim, that this great Law is unjust? Did not God Himself say, "The soul that sinneth it shall surely die." And is not the Law, when received, and deliberately broken, sufficient to mete out full punishment?

Only he who is, in his own nature, unjust and treacherous and unfaithful can claim that the Law is unjust. Moreover, what can be more utterly condemnable than for a man, knowing part of the truths concerning the Soul, to obtain, through the virtue of hits most Sacred Vows, instructions and books belonging to a Mystic Fraternity, and then, after obtaining them on promise to work for that Fraternity, deliberately to betray his trust, deliberately to break his promise, and why? Simply because the Fraternity and the Masters thereof do not see fit to do as he wants done. Remember, the Fraternity and its teachers can obey only the Hierarchic Powers, and not any man, nor any member, no matter how great the member may be.

When we turn from Egypt to Greece, we find still greater development, in so far as man is concerned. There we find perfection in the arts, perfection in man himself; for man, physically, mentally, and socially, with his love for the beautiful, had reached very near to the gods. And only when selfish interest began to usurp the love of the beautiful, did Greece start to fall. And in Greece, as in Egypt, it was during the time in which the true Priesthood held sway that she was at her greatest. With the fall of the Priesthood, came the fall of the nation itself, just as had happened in Egypt.

Reference here is not made to a selfish priesthood, which meddles in politics, and which would rule its adherents with a rod of iron, taking from them their liberty and freedom of thought. We refer to that Mighty Priesthood or Initiates, which ruled through knowledge and which taught others, all its Neophytes, to "know themselves." The remnant of this mighty Fraternity has continued in existence throughout the ages, and it still continues to exist, beginning once more to draw many to itself, many who are now under training, in order that they may become one with the Mystic Fraternity, and become teachers and healers of mankind, teaching mankind the Divine Law, the Law that shall make them free from fear, free from the selfish self, which always ends in destruction.

Thus, a Mystic writer has said: "Universal history not only demonstrates an advance of the human race in civilization, but still more in the development of different intellectual powers in all directions, in which the primeval ideas of truth and goodness, of beauty and of truth, come forth from the subjective ground into the objective revelation. The mightiest nations are always those who, in general development, most purely and perfectly manifest a peculiar (Mystic) spirit, or the substance of some particular idea. People who have not impressed upon them these primeval ideas in a permanent form are destitute of history, and disappear like shadows on the arena of the world."

This is certainly true. They have been many nations; but most of them have been forgotten. Only of those nations, those ages, in which there existed a mighty Priesthood, truly called Occult, or Mystic, have we any great record. Among these nations, we find the Egyptian, the Grecian, and the Greco-Roman. Further: "These people have raised themselves above all others by their intellectual stamina, and with a characteristic strength, and have planted on a certain elevation of development the focus of an advanced knowledge, which can never more vanish from history, but must forever pass on to a fresh posterity, and be again brought forward by it, but only in a new form, and more varied and entwined with the roots of its peculiar ,strength of life."

This is true, and, America, once part of the ancient Egyptian continent, bids fair to take up these ideas, this training, of the Ancients, which made the ancient nations such wonderful powers, and which helped them to reach such a wonderful state of development in all lines that enable man to become a better and a happier being. Further: "When the human spirit possessed no higher wisdom than the earthly and the human, than that which reason and the light of nature gave it, nature was a sealed book- a Babel. Man had wholly fallen from his empires; his sense and language were confused; no consciousness of the real object of life remained to him, nor of the true use of means. Man was blind, and deaf, and lame, as it regarded the kingdom of nature."

This is the state in which we find most of mankind at the present day, knowing nothing of the Mystic, nothing of the Soul, only a little of that which belongs to the body. Thus Nature is a sealed book to him. Of another such age, Jacob Boehme, the mystic, wrote: "But the soul of the old Adam lusted after the lordship of the outer rule, and his will was sundered from the unity of God, and carried away in the dominion of this world; so that this was converted into a monstrosity. The true spirit withered; the light of God was extinguished; and the divine idea became benumbed and dead to him. To this spirit now came

THE AETH MYSTERY

Jesus; and as he assumed human nature, to restore it, he brought back again the light into the darkness. In this light stands the soul again in original fatherland, as in her first days, when the spirit of God wrought in her. She stands there in vision, and may inquire into all things; and she understands the language of nature, and works with her strength. In delusion- that of Adam- there is no perfection; the spirit of God in His Son (the Christos) must be the guide, otherwise he stands in an outward mystery, as in the outward heaven of the stars, but not in the Divine Magic School, which consists only in a simple, childlike spirit. The outward guide- theoretic reason- works only in a glass; but the inner sense, directed of God, shines into the soul; and, therefore, the choice stands with God; he who comprehends the heavenly school will become a Magus- a creator out of self-knowledge- without weariness running; and even if he must greatly exert himself, yet is he penetrated by God, and will be impelled by the Holy Spirit (the Illuminated Soul.)"

This, we of the Aeth Fraternity hold as a sacred truth; and it is this building of the Illuminated Soul, with all its native strength and power, that we would teach to those who are truly and sincerely interested.

PRELIMINARY TRAINING

The first, or preliminary, training in the Aeth School has been called the Healing Course. This, for the reason that the power used in healing the ills' of mankind is the very same power that is used for all other purposes, only the power is used in another way when for any other than a healing purpose. The development of the mind, the body, and the soul is the same in all cases. It, therefore, follows that the development of power is also the same.

This Aeth power in man can be brought forth only

through certain drills, exercises, modes of living, and, above all, through the use of Sacred Mantrams, which help the Neophyte to come into direct communication with the Aeth World, and therefore to receive the Aeth Forces, or the Divine Fire.

The old Philosophers well taught that the air, like all things in nature, is double- that is, it is negative and positive, male and female- and it is in the knowledge of how to breathe 'that man is able to draw in the Aeth Forces, which give him all power. The air that we breathe is double in all cases. It takes upon itself the earth elements and makes man an entirely carnal, lustful being, degraded, in many cases, and non immortal; and, on the other hand, the air will take on the elements of the Heavenly Fires, and give man power, strength, and Immortality. It is for the Neophyte to choose which it shall be; and, as he chooses, he makes use of the air according to his choice.

That the old Philosopher-Initiate's knew the secret that is in the air, and knew of the power of the Aeth, and how, to take this so as to develop all power, can readily be seen by those who read, and understand, these philosophers. Thus we read:

"The air has its positive and negative, its male and female. It takes up into itself all earthly elements, develops, in eternal changes, all power in itself, and begets innumerable children in undiminished youth and beauty. Juno is the sister and spouse of Jupiter. Among the natural philosophers, Juno means the lower atmosphere, in which the clouds float and the rainbow appears. She is the eldest daughter of Kronos, and sister of Zeus (God). Oceanos and Tethys brought her up, when the all-power Zeus thrust Kronos under the earth; that is, the vapor, ascending from the Sea, and the waters mix themselves in the lower atmosphere. According to Ovid, Hera was swallowed up by her father with the rest of his children, and again vomited forth. The eagle soaring to the sun is the bird of Jupiter; while the earthly, color-reflecting peacock is the attendant of Juno.

Vulcan, a son of Jupiter, received the lord,ship of the subterranean. Like Fire, which at first appears as a feeble spark, was Vulcan at birth. He was weak, ugly, ailing, slow and limping; but when grown up, and requiring strength, possessed of a sinewy neck and strong chest. He built a house for himself, which was imperishable, and therein he had his workshop, with his anvil and his bellows, which without hands worked at his command. The Cyclops, the remnant of the original powers of nature, children of Urania and Gaea, forged for Zeus lightnings and thunderbolts, dwelling in the volcanic caves. Vulcan appears among the Pelasgic gods, the Samothracian Cabiri, as the symbol of electric power, and out of the common workshop of Hephaestos and Athene is Prometheus said to have taken the life-giving power."

In the above is contained not only the mystery of creation, but the mystery of the soul, low born and weak, then gradually gaining strength until it knows the Mystery of Fire, of Youth, and of Immortality. Read this, time and again; and gradually you will see the Mystery of the breath, that there are two forces in the air, one that is earthly, giving life only to the body, the other heavenly, divine, giving health, strength, power and Immortality.

In the preliminary course in the Aeth School, covering one year of training and development, and including all Sacred Mantrams, the mystery of breath is fully taught, and man receives information concerning the Aeth World, or Sphere, that Sphere wherein dwells the power for health, for strength, for power, for youth, and for Immortality; and the Neophyte is taught how to come into contact with, and how to draw in, this Aeth Fire, the Life-Giving Power.

THE AETH MYSTERY

This section of the instructions gives a statement as to the foundation of the Aeth Philosophy and the reason for the Aeth World, which may be considered as a sphere filled with Vital Fire. The student is here taught how to come into touch with this Sphere, and how to draw the Life Fire to himself. There is a Philosophy in the Aeth Priesthood teachings. No system can exist without a philosophy, because, without such a philosophy, there is no foundation whereon to build, and it is admitted that the Philosophy of the Aeth School' is the most sound of any philosophy known to the student at this day. Man can not reach Immortality after he passes to the beyond. Man must reach it while in the earth life. For this very reason the earth life is given to him.

It is the same with the Aeth World and its powers. Man must come into contact with it, and draw therefrom, now, and not some time after the reaper has taken him and forwarded him to the Beyond. It must not be thought by the student that, in these lessons, only breathing is taught. Nothing could be farther from the truth. In truth, the Neophyte is taught the correct system of breathing, but that is only one part of the work. Correct breathing, without knowledge and making use of the Sacred Mantrams, would accomplish nothing except possibly to strengthen the body. It is through a correct system of living, breathing, and the Holy Invocations that man can come into contact with, and draw in these Aeth Fires.

The first three lessors are confined entirely to the teachings of the Philosophy concerning the Aeth World. In these lessons are given the reasons and the wherefore. Herein, also, are taught the philosophical beliefs; but, more than this practical instructions are given, instructions as to how to live, how to breathe, and, above all else, the Sacred Mantrams that are to be used during this time of training.

THE MYSTERY OF THE AETH

In the fourth lesson, the Mystery of the Aeth is explained and further instructions are given. The physical age, the mental age, these have passed, and man has entered into the third and highest stage of development. This is the Soul Age, the Age of Illumination; and it remains to be seen whether man will take up the work belonging to this age and thus find Immortality or whether he will, like different civilizations, pay no heed to the time, and die out, as did past civilizations because they could not, or would not, read the signs of the times, so that the result was decay and death to such civilizations. We, of the Brotherhood, believe that mankind, generally considered, is awakening very fast, and that it will not miss the opportunities held out, but will grasp them and thus draw to itself all power, and end in Immortality and the Sublime Millennium.

Lesson five continues the instructions concerning the Mystery of the Aeth. In this lesson there is an additional Sacred Mantram, which is to be used in the work in order that man may come closer to his God, by manifesting the powers and the virtues expressed by the Godhead.

THE AETH FORCE

The Aeth Force is the greatest force in the universe. It is the greatest, highest, and most ,sublime force that can be known to man. The mysteries of magnetism, of electricity, have not yet become known to man. These forces are now used daily, they are harnessed and used; but man knows not the power of these servants of his. But even these forces are only the material side of the greater Aeth Forces. And, different from electricity,

14

different from magnetism, the Neophyte, through obedience to the instructions of the School, is enabled to make use of these forces and also to see them as he sees a fire; and for this reason he is better prepared to handle them, and to make use of them, than he is to make use of electricity. Very little has been known of the Life Forces; and, in late years, very few discoveries have been made that give us light on the subject. All that is known today, and much more, was known to many of the old philosophers; and many of the life processes were made use of by them, and these are lost to, or hidden from, the materialists of the present age.

God gave man certain powers; moreover, he gave man the right to gain other powers. He gave man life, and he gave him also the power to draw in still more of this life force. If man does not use it, or if he remains ignorant, then he has no one to blame but himself. We, of the Aeth School, hold that it is the subtle Aeth that underlies all life. We further hold that, through a system of living and training, the body may be so prepared as to be enabled to draw in more of this Aeth Force, to draw it in and to store it up, so as to use it for whatever purpose is desired; and we hold, further, that all men who are willing to obey can accomplish this within a short time.

The Life Principle, the Spirit of God, never ceases to exist, never becomes less. If man passes on, if he becomes ill and dies, it simply shows that he has ceased to draw in, and to store, this Life Force. In the Aeth instructions, man is taught how continually to draw in this Life Force. He is taught how to come into touch with the Aeth Forces, and thus to gain health, strength, and the power to accomplish. But that which is of greater importance is the fact that, just as he succeeds in doing this, he will also be building the Immortal Soul.

It is utterly impossible for the evil man to make use of

this power; for k is impossible for him to come into touch with the Hierarchic Powers unless his desires are pure. It therefore naturally follows that whoever enters into and heeds not only obtains more of life, but more of goodness also, and with this comes the Immortalization of the Soul.

Lesson seven in the series continues the explanation and instructions concerning the Aeth Force, and gives additional Sacred Invocations, which will help the student on the way, preparing him still further for the highest work that can be given to any man by anyone. We might go on indefinitely as to what this Aeth Force is, and concerning the training of the first year; but we believe not much would be accomplished by so doing. We therefore give only an outline of the work, stating the fact that there are 24 lessons in the preliminary course, covering a period of one year, after which is taken up the course in the Highest Work known to man in the Mystic field.

GENERAL OUTLINE OF THE AETH TRAINING

The Aeth is a force in nature emanating from the Aeth World. The existence of the Aeth Sphere near the sun, and the wonderful potency of its emanations, were known and understood by the Egyptian Priesthood many centuries ago. Instructions regarding how to use the Aeth Forces were carefully guarded by the Priests of the Temples, and were never imparted openly. Only those qualified by sincere nobility and purity of purpose were admitted to the Inner Court in which the Aeth Philosophy was explained. The Laws of the Aeth Philosophy, handed down from the Highest Egyptian Priesthood of Initiates, have been preserved in their purity, and are now offered to you under the auspices of the Aeth Priesthood.

The Aeth is a power that may be employed accurately and intelligently. The Aeth is a power that may be employed in the healing of others, in the healing of the self, and in furthering laudable interests in any work that may be near and dear to the heart of man, provided such work has nothing to do with the destruction of life or with hate and malice. It is a power that may be applied to the practical needs of life in all its varied departments. It was this Aeth Force that the Master Jesus so well understood, and so adeptly employed in his work as healer and teacher.

It must be emphasized that these lessons give not only a philosophy, but practical instructions, instructions which the Neophyte can follow. Their aim goes deeper than merely to give facts and to impart knowledge. It is a course of instructions and training that differs from other systems in that it has for its distinctive purposes the development of greater power within the Neophyte, power which can be used not only in healing the ills of others, in self-healing, in the drawing in of health, strength, and youthful vitality, but also for every other known purpose, for every purpose for which the Mystic might use a mighty power. It is not simply a healing course, a healer's training.

It is so called, as already stated, simply because the force used in true healing is the same force used for every other Mystic or Occult purpose, but in a different manner. Avail yourself of these lessons, and you will see for yourself that they are specifically a system of personal training- training calculated to develop power of mind, body, and soul, calculated to establish your connection with the Aeth World; calculated to develop the ability to take in, to absorb, and to retain the Aeth Forces- the ability to direct the Aeth Vitality to the organism of ethers or to the conditions of your own being. But, remember, the Aeth Power, when once developed, is by no means limited to the work of healing. It may be directed effectively into any desired channel, and may be used for any worthy purpose.

THE AETH MYSTERY

If you have ability as a nurse, this is an excellent system of training, enabling you to impart hope, courage, and healing vibrations to those to whom you minister. Your opportunity is even greater in some respects than that of the professional healer. Being with the patient at a time of special need, when the body is sensitive to every touch, when the mind is sensitive to every word and even to every thought, you are in a position to give most potent suggestions, and to be an avenue for the transference of Aeth Forces.

But heed well the fact that these instructions are not limited to those who are to become healers and nurses by profession. They are especially applicable to you if your health is impaired, if you are yourself in need of building up physical health and vitality. Remember, too, that enrollment for these lessons entitles you to the personal attention and advice of an Aeth Priest and Healer, under whose care you may consider yourself as long as treatment is needed. The Aeth Philosophy is founded on the principle that physical health, strength, and vitality are of fundamental importance to everyone. Consequently, it gives detailed attention to matters of diet, breathing, bathing, exercise, thought control, and other requisites of physical health, and adapts the instructions to your personal needs. If you are lacking in strength and vigor, the Aeth Priesthood promises without the shadow of a doubt to help you to establish conditions of health and strength. Again, the Aeth Philosophy will be of inestimable value to any person that aspires to worthy service in any department of life. Who does not wish to be efficient and competent in whatever position he holds?

Just as soon as this first year's preliminary course of instructions is finished, then the student will be at once started with the higher work and training. This training will then be still more personal, still more individual, than the first course, because it has to do absolutely and entirely with himself and his own Soul and Soul Powers. The work following the first course is that which has been given to the Neophyte in the Egyptian, Grecian, and other Temples of Initiation, and is the highest that can be given to mankind. It may here be stated that, when the Higher Work of the Sacred Art is taken up, it is not supposed that the work as taught in the first course should be given up. On the contrary, all things taught regarding breathing, bathing, exercise, etc., should be continued until they become fixed habits of life, as each additional day these instructions, this life, is followed, will add additional life and power.

THE AETH FORCES

P. B. Randolph once wrote these lines:

"Some people there be in this section of the civilized area of the earth who can not imagine anything of magic power or magnetic ability in the human soul, either latent or active, nor indeed any other superior power or energies at all, than such as find their field of use in heaping up wealth through the diabolic magic of rascality on change, in trade and elsewhere, or in seeking to gratify tastes brutal at their bases, and lusts foul enough to shame Satan."

That which Randolph wrote more than fifty years ago is as true today a,s it was then; and this booklet, giving information concerning the Aeth Priesthood and its Aeth teachings, is not for such as believe in the type of magic indicated above, but for those who believe that there are more things in this world than the material mind can know and understand, and for such as have, through experiences of one kind or another, learned to know that there are hidden potencies and energies in the human soul, so great as to be unbelievable by those who have not yet come to know.

THE AETH MYSTERY

INCREASING THE LIFE FORCES

One of the most important, because basic, teachings of the Fraternity is that which has to do with the opening up, the filling up, of the reservoirs of life. That this has been the dream of the old philosophers and Initiates, there is no longer any question, and that many of them did actually find the secret of the prolongation of life, is also beyond question, for the reason that many of them had life beyond the years usually allotted to man. Moreover, we see many of them so weak as seemingly not to be able to live another twenty-four hours; but twenty-four hour,s thereafter they were as strong as ever, and there were no signs of the cessation of life.

And why is this? Simply because they had learned the secret of being able to take in the Aeth or Dynamic Forces, or Energies, from the Aeth Spaces, and had learned how to come into touch, or direct communication, with the Hierarchic Powers, or that department of these Hierarchic Powers which had guard over, or control of, the Aeth or Dynamic Life Forces.

SPECIFIC ENERGIES

Once the Dynamic Life Forces, or Energies, are under control to a certain extent, so that man knows that he is taking in more of these energies than he is using up, thereby assuring him of health and long life, the next important thing necessary to him who is on the Path of Initiation is the knowledge and the power not only to have specific energies, but to prolong this specific energy to such an extent that he is assured both of the knowledge of accomplishing this very thing and of the possession of a sufficient degree of specific power to enable him to be successful in the department of life in which he is interested. The Aeth Fraternity not only teaches its Neophytes that there are such

THE AETH MYSTERY

Specific Powers and Energies, but teaches them how to develop such powers, how to store the energy, having it when needed, so that, even while it is being used, man has the power to draw in, through the Divine Secret of Breath, more energy and more power than he is actually losing, thus assuring a surplus of this Dynamic Energy and Power.

This can not be accomplished by any man unless he knows not only the secret of the Sacred Breath, but also the Divine Mantrams, or Divine Invocations, with which, or through which, he comes in touch with the Hierarchic Powers of the Aeth Spaces. This the Aeth Priesthood teaches. This it has always taught its Neophytes; and this it will continue to teach as part of its work.

THE CHANGE OF NATURE

In this age, as in past ages, we find many who are a contradiction within themselves. They desire one thing, but are attuned to another; and thus their dual nature is in constant conflict. It is this fight continually taking place which forever bars them from peace, happiness, and contentment; but, when this is removed, and the dual nature is harmonized, then they find strength, peace, happiness, and natural powers. This change can only be brought about through a process of transmutation, changing the hostile part of the dual nature, and harmonizing it with the harmonious nature. Only through the Aereal influences, can this change be brought about; and here it is again where the help of the Hierarchic Forces are required, which can be had through the proper understanding of the Law. These Laws are thoroughly taught by the Fraternity; and it is through the understanding of these Laws that many who were failures have been helped to success- a success that is not alone material, but spiritual as well- for success, to be real, must be of the threefold being, and this can not be had so long as the dual nature is continually at war.

THE SUBLIME LOVE NATURE

It is an admitted fact that the true love nature of man almost universally is weak and degraded, that life, as it has been lived the past many centuries, has had a tendency to degrade the love nature, in many cases killing it out, while making the carnal, the passion nature supreme. It is also admitted that the love nature, often called the God nature, because it is the Creative Nature, is the Base, the very Foundation, of all true and lasting power.

This the Aeth Priesthood recognizes as true; and it is, therefore, one of the foundation teachings and training, to develop this nature in man, bringing it to a natural, normal, Divine Potency. It has been said by many great teachers, "Where dwells Love, there dwells God." The Aeth Priesthood holds this as a truism, so much so that it is fundamental with the Fraternity; and centuries of experience in teaching has proved to the teachers the absolute truth of the statement made.

THE HELP OF THE SPACES

One of the greatest desires of the old teachers- one which they made special effort to realize in the very beginning of the Great Work- was, as they stated, to have "mental dalliance with the Powers of Space."

New Thought, so-called, has been enabled to do much good with its power of mind; but even New Thought is only a glimpse of the vast power that can be used by man. Mankind, at present, has been taught only the power of his own mind when it is properly developed; but mankind is in total ignorance of the immense and awful power that may be his to use for good, if he

THE AETH MYSTERY

learns both to use his own mind and mental powers properly and
also to bring his own mental forces into harmony, so as to use,
not only his own, but also the help and the assistance of the
Powers of the Spaces. These powers of the Spaces, we, of the
Aeth Fraternity, have rightly termed the Hierarchic Powers. Not
only are they mental, but they include all the powers of nature,
all the Ruling Powers of every department of nature; and
therefore we call them the Hierarchic Powers. The Neophyte is
taught how he may come into touch with these Hierarchic
Powers and Forces, and how he may have their powers to
reinforce his own.

CULTIVATION OF WILL

Much has been said concerning the cultivation of the
Will; but few have been enabled to teach the secret of power.

We of the Fraternity, having at our command the
teachings of the old and the new masters, know that that which
has been taught elsewhere is not even a beginning of that which
is held by the Fraternity; because the Fraternity does not go into
theory, but gives the Neophyte the actual practice, degree after
degree, until he has learned the three mighty powers, powers
held as sacred by all Initiates of the Fraternity, and rightly named
Volantia, Decretism, and Posism.

Practice after practice follows, until the Neophyte has
mastered the different stages of the power, and has gained not
only the knowledge of how, but the ability to do.

SPECIAL POWERS FOR SPECIAL PURPOSES

It has always been held by the Fraternity that there
resides a power in the true man, which, when developed and
understood, may be used in the Charging of certain substances.

23

THE AETH MYSTERY

These substances, being agents, will retain that specific power, and will, when coming into contact with the person that is negative or deficient in that special power, become a part of him and strengthen him. That this power has been used by the old Priesthood even in the Roman Church can not be denied, that it has been practically lost, is also beyond contradiction. The Fraternity holds that this power may be developed by all men. The Fraternity further maintains that it has always taught the principles of developing this power, and that it now continues to teach them to its Neophytes.

This making use of the Aethic power is not new, but has been one of the principles that has been possessed by the Aeth Fraternity ever since it,s foundation, long before the Egyptian Empire was at its height. This principle of developing and using the Aethic power by means of properly charged substances, was employed by Pythagoras, by Paracelsus, by Von Helmont. It was used, in an inferior form, by Mesmer; and, by means of it, Mesmer, though not an Initiate, was enabled to make wonderful and almost unbelievable cures. But this power of Charging substances and beings is not only of use in the cure of the ills of mankind, but it can be used for every other purpose; and it is this power which can often be used in the saving of a weak or erring man from crimes and vices. Its application is unlimited.

THE ORIENTAL BREAST DRILL

Of the Oriental Breast Drill, nothing can be said in a booklet of this nature, which, though placed only before those who are interested in the Sacred Philosophy, is, nevertheless, for general circulation. It may be stated, however, that, through the teachings and the application of the teachings as given in these private instructions, many families have been saved from disruption. Men who were growing away from their wives have been reclaimed, and women who were growing away from the husband and father have returned to the family fold. And all this, not through the power Of external agencies or force, but through the knowledge gained of their own being, and through the power developed within themselves by means of the Sacred Breath Drill. This secret is of Oriental origin, as the western mind, though intellectual, is not of the,sunny nature as is the mind of the Oriental people, and seldom discovers those secrets of being which are the common knowledge of the high caste Oriental. It must not be understood that the Aeth Philosophy teaches an Oriental Philosophy pure and simple, or a Philosophy of Negativism. Nothing of the kind; but, having been founded in the Egyptian country, centuries ago, it naturally follows that the Aeth Philosophy retains the teachings and the practices that have, throughout the ages proved to be exact and constructive in results, although it discards all negative and destructive tendencies prevalent among Oriental philosophies.

THE PRACTICES OF POWER

Again, we refer to one who was of our own time, and who said that this practice was "to culture the power of direct, impressive, magnetic presence, for general, affectional, or business purposes." The higher culture includes the whole man, the threefold being; and it recognize the threefold man, when equally developed, as the true, the complete man. No man can be truly man whose affectional nature is either imperfectly developed or cold. It is the Love Nature, the Great Center, whence come the Magnetic Waves, which constitute Magnetic Attraction. And, unless one has these Magnetic Waves, success in no department of nature can be perfect. And, unless this affectional being, this Love Nature, is developed, normal, and natural, man is an imperfect being.

But the more fully this nature is developed, the more fully and completely will the Great Center radiate the Magnetic,

THE AETH MYSTERY

the Attractive Waves. And, what is still more true, and of greater importance, is the fact that, as this Great Center, this Love Nature, is developed, man becomes more truly man, more truly the being that God intended him to be. "The true man is too much of a man to do anything which is not manly."

But, if the affectional nature is developed at the expense of the physical and the Soul natures, there will be a conflict, a weakness; and man, though fully man as regards his love nature, will be weak morally, because the physical and the soul beings will not have the strength to resist the desires of the affectional nature. Thereby, the affectional nature becomes one-sided, and this may result in acts which are not what they should be. Thus it is, that the Aeth Fraternity insists on a threefold development, and follows the system of training practiced by the Ancient Initiates, which has always proved a success.

AFFILIATION OF WILLS

The most powerful of all practices, and that which has, in part, already been referred to, is the affiliation of the will of man, called the earth-will, with the Will-assembly of the Spaces, with the Hierarchic Powers. It is here where the highest form of Will has its beginning and its ending; for the human will, well-trained, affiliated with that of the Hierarchic Will-assembly, is proof against all things, and man, through this affiliation, becomes as one of the gods. Nor do we utter anything profane when we make this statement; for it has been uttered by our Initiates in all ages. God Himself said, "Man has become as one of the gods." This training is not difficult to him who is truly willing to try; but, to the weakling, to the one who desires power without working for power, it becomes impossible.

Nothing is denied to him who truly WILLS. It therefore follows that he who is truly willing to will will also be willing to

THE AETH MYSTERY

act, to live, and whose lives will know the power of his specific form of living.

OTHER POWERS AND SPACES

It must not be understood that the Will alone has Spaces in the Aeth Spheres, and that there are Hierarchic Powers over Will alone. On the contrary, just as there are Hierarchic Powers of Will so there are Hierarchic Powers of Divine Passion, of the Will-Love-Energy. There are Centers with their Hierarchic Powers over every department of Life and in every Department of Nature ; and he who knows can come into touch with these Centers, these Hierarchic Powers.

AFFILIATION WITH CENTERS

The Fraternity has ever taught the possibility, and the means, of drawing power and energy from the four Great Centers. This is not altogether an Egyptian teaching, but was the secret of the Greek-Chaldaic people; and this power of drawing verve from the four Centers was known as the Greek-Chaldaic principle of Austro-fusion. These Centers have to do with the nature of man- that is, with his principal natures- and cover the four great departments of life. Only a working knowledge and the will to do is required by the Neophyte in order to make use of this secret.

POSITIVENESS OF SOUL

It may be stated as an absolute and uncontradictable fact that no man can become an Initiate unless he is first able to develop a positiveness of Soul. This may be accomplished through purely mental practices. But, like all mental powers, it is then a cold power, and does not attract or draw to as it would if positiveness of Soul is developed through the Love Energies.

27

THE AETH MYSTERY

The Aeth Fraternity teaches both of these systems, but it holds that, as man's true love nature is a part of the God nature, it is far better to develop all Soul Powers, including positiveness of Soul, through the Love-energies, than it is to develop the Soul through purely mental practices. The Soul that has gained Positiveness, especially if it has been gained through the Love-energies, is practically invincible. Moreover, it is a great, powerful, sublime attracting Center, a Center that attracts the good and the true, as does the magnet attract the needle; and this is desirable in every instance

INTENSIFICATION

It is an established fact that the man who is lukewarm in his interests is not a man who accomplishes great things. But the man who is intense in his desires, in his love, and who, being intense (Polarized), is willing to make any necessary sacrifice in order to accomplish- he is the one who will accomplish. For there is no power in heaven or on earth that can gainsay the Mighty Will of him who says, "I Will" and who holds to that intense resolution, no matter what may come, and who is willing to make any sacrifice in order to accomplish. It is such of whom Jesus, the Great Initiate, said: "He dies but to gain his life", "He fails but to conquer." For, though it may seem that, for the time, such an one loses his all, and is reduced to the lowest ranks of existence, at the moment he is so reduced the fates themselves will turn to him and give him aid, and he will begin to climb upward and upward until he has reached the summit. And here is the Great Law: "Just as he had to sacrifice and suffer in order to win, so will he, in like intensity, enjoy and live; for the intensity of suffering and the willingness to sacrifice are but the measure of the possibility and the capability of enjoying and succeeding."

It therefore follows that we can readily judge the tree by its fruits. We can judge the possibility, or the power, of good in a

28

man by what he is willing to suffer, willing to sacrifice, in order to obtain the thing he desires. That is the law. And all the Hierarchies of the Spaces are arrayed with the man who says, "I Will", and who will do in spite of what comes; for the Hierarchic Powers are ever with the man who promises to do and who does as he promises. This is the law. Nothing worth while in heaven or on earth is gained without the making of some sacrifice. The things we buy, for which we have ready money, never bring us the satisfaction that do those things for which we had to save and to suffer. We know the value of the things for which we suffer. They are part of our lives; aye, part of our blood is in them.

SECRETS OF THE SPACES

In spite of all that has been said against Clear-Seeing there is such a thing as Clear-Seeing. The very fact that a thing is counterfeited proves that there is a thing that is genuine. A Master has said that part of the powers belonging to the Initiate are these:

"To penetrate the secrets of the lower Spacial Worlds, a power called Suvoyance.

To penetrate the formidable Sphere of the middle Spaces, called Zorvoyance.

To attain the road leading to the Ineffable Beyond, called Aethaevoyance."

It is this last to which the true Initiate desires to reach. And he does reach to these Spaces when he becomes Master of the Soul Ceremonies, when he masters the Sacred Mantrams that are taught by the Fraternity. This last is truly the secret religion of the Ancient Initiates, because it teaches a Specific Form of Invocations, which are at once powerful prayers of the highest and most sublime form, and appeals to the Hierarchic Powers of the Special Departments in the Universe in order to obtain the help that is necessary. Religion is of the Soul. So is all true and lasting power. The work of the two therefore becomes one.

THE LIFE SECRET

The greatest secret possessed by Paracelsus, the great healer, and the one who has given the modern physician many of his most important medicines, was the secret of Vitalizing foods, medicines, drinks, clothing, etc., with a Specific, Dynamic Power which would, when taken by a person, endow that person with just so much power, the full amount with which the specific article had been Charged. So great was the power of Vitalization possessed by Paracelsus that in many cases he instantly healed, with one dose of medicine, diseases which had been of long standing, and which had resisted the combined power of many physicians.

This has justly been termed the Grand Life Secret, because it is, in many instances, the means of saving life; in others, it is the means of prolonging life for many years and making the prolonged life greater than was the former life.

THE DEFEAT OF NEGATIVISM

In the present age, when mankind has been taught, and believes in, the destructive power over other minds, is is well to know the laws that help man to build the Electric Auric Ring, which, when thrown around one's self or around another, is the means of turning away any adverse or hostile influence that may have been cast against one. The Positive Soul has no fear of such things, because positiveness of Soul is a protection in itself. But those who fear this adverse or hostile force have no such protection, and cannot protect themselves. It is therefore highly necessary that others should know how to protect those who are fearful of hostile influences, in order to free them from that which fear has placed upon them.

The filling of the air around one's self with the Aeth Forces is not a difficult matter, and such an Auric Ring is a protection against every evil that may have been cast forth by a mind that is full of hate and malice. The Initiate does not fear these things, but, only the few being Initiates, the millions will suffer through fear, which is but a form of negativeness.

THE FACULTIES OF THE SOUL

The whole work of Initiation, or training in the Aeth School, is to awaken, to train, and to develop the Soul Powers- It is a process of practice, which will, degree by degree, awaken the slumbering Soul, bring all its powers to manifestation, and make it master of the Aeth Processes, step by step, until Mastership is reached. And this process of self-development includes in it, and develops harmoniously, the power to attract to one's self innumerable Aethic, Aerial, and Invisible assistants. This the modern school terms Hierarchic Invocation, or Invocation of Hierarchic Powers. It was termed by the Ancient School Arsaphism. No Initiation is complete unless it accomplishes this, and the Aeth Fraternity claims to teach the methods. It further claims that whoso lives and obeys the teachings must come into the power that such 'living confers. This it can well claim, for each and every man is no more and no less than the life that he leads makes him to be.

SPECIFIC PARTS OF THE HIGHER OCCULT TRAINING

THOUGHT

All Masters of the past have admitted and taught that

thought is the base of all true life; that Immortality is not possible to man unless he first begins to think that there is such a thing as Immortality, and then gradually begins to work in harmony with the Divine Law, thereby upbuilding, the Divine Spark within himself, and thus not only having a body with which to move and act, but a soul as truly conscious of its existence as is the body. The Aeth Fraternity in its instructions and training does not go into theory, but it gives practical instructions as to just what to do and how to do it. Thus, it teaches the Neophyte that the first work in the Great Art is Image Formation, because by this process that which the Neophyte desires to do or to accomplish is formed in his mind as an image; and this is held to the exclusion of all else, until the desire has become realized.

To the novice this may seem to be a very difficult matter, but in reality it is not hard to do, because the training and the instructions are so clear, so to the point, that no mistake can be made by one who is sincere.

SECOND LOGOS

Image Formation is only the very first step in the Great Art It is but the 'a' in the Great Alphabet. Following the First Logos we have the Second Logos, which is the work of Vivifying, or Giving Life to, the Image formed, or the sending forth of the attracting power, which will bring about desired results. This is a little more difficult than is the first practice, because it is the actual giving of life to an inanimate object, to an image formed by the Soul and the actual seeing it as it should be when it becomes materialized.

Previous training is necessary to qualify the Neophyte to enter upon these exercises- It must not be thought that these practices, this higher training, is given to the beginner. Long

THE AETH MYSTERY

before these Drills are given, the student will already have been taught the Sacred Mantrams whereby he has developed the body and trained the mind in preparation for this higher work. Image Vivification is of the utmost importance, and no man truly becomes an Initiate, a Priest of the Mysteries, until he has accomplished this work. And he can accomplish it if he is willing to do his part, willing not only to read and study, but willing to practice and willing to act.

THIRD LOGOS

Once man has mastered the practice of Image Formation and Image Vivification, or giving life to the image formed, then he is ready for the Third Logos, which is that of the projection of the Imaged and Vivified Creation of his mind. This is one of the most important parts of the Great Work, though it is not so difficult as is that of Formation and Vivification, because he will have become more nearly the Master than he was before he started the work, and, though apparently each step is more difficult than the former one, to him it is not so difficult because he has grown since the start was made by him, and as he nears the goal the Work becomes easier. These three Logi contain all power and all mastery. Through these it is possible to influence all things, both that which is near and that which is far away. Distance cannot interfere with the influence of the mind.

SILENCE

In the Hall of Silence man accomplishes the Great Work. For this reason the old Masters and Initiates taught that it is necessary to know, to will, to dare, and to keep silent. Of these four, silence is as important as any of the other three because it is in silence that all great work is accomplished, and he who talks does not know, and he who knows does not talk. Silently must man begin the work, for it is a work that concerns only himself.

THE AETH MYSTERY

Only he himself should know what he is about; the world in general has nothing to do with it. When Mastership has been reached, then it is that he may use his powers, his influences for good and for the good of humanity, but even then it is not necessary for him to talk concerning himself and the work, unless he is appointed in a position where he is to give information, not otherwise.

All nature works silently and in secret, and he who most closely follows nature is sure to have more of the power and strength that is possessed by nature. The Great Fraternity herself is a proof of this fact. For centuries she had remained silent, and often men knew not that she continued to exist, knew not that here and there were men and women who, though following a specific profession, were also following the Great Work and using their power and influence for the good of mankind generally. These men- these Initiates- did not care whether any man knew of their work or not. It was sufficient to them that they were fulfilling their destiny in spite of everything to the contrary, and they found that their work, the things accomplished, were complete recompense for the sacrifices made, for the energy given and for the self-denial necessary. Here let it be said that the greater the self denial made by the Neophyte or the Master, the greater is the return in peace and power. For without labor and without sacrifice nothing is accomplished in the Great Art.

THE HALL OF SILENCE

Moreover, it is actually in the Hall of Silence that the Soul of the Neophyte meet,s two worlds. It is there where the one ends and the other begins. It is there where he stands with one foot in the visible world and with the ether in the so-called Invisible World. There it is that the Soul first tastes of the Immortal Fire. There that the eyes first behold the Mystery of the Fire which burns on the Sacred Altar, and which is reflected

34

upon the screen through the medium of the Drill. The Neophyte in this Hall needs patience; for just as the rose plant needs careful watching and time to grow before it will put forth a bud, and then gradually open into a full-blown rose, so does the man need time and careful watching in order that the Soul may grow and show forth its Divine Fire. But he who has patience and who is truly sincere will be fully rewarded for every sacrifice made in order to attain.

MANIFESTATION

When once the first Three Logi are mastered, and when these are practiced, then comes the manifestation, or the gradual coming into existence of that which was formed, vivified, and projected. It must not be thought that this is accomplished in a day, though it is possible where the Will of the Neophyte is strong enough and where the Arts have been perfectly mastered, to bring into immediate existence some things, as, for instance, when the Neophyte desires to heal some one who has faith. In that instance the perfect image of the whole being may be formed; this may be Vivified with perfect Life; this may be projected and manifestations may take place at once.

There are other instances, other works, in which this may be accomplished; but where the desire is for the creation of a power or a faculty time may be required in order that such power or such faculty may grow and develop. However simple this work may seem it is yet a work that needs great practice and careful watching, and the Neophyte needs the guidance of the most nearly perfect and the most interested instructor if he would succeed fully. And not only does he need such an instructor, but on his part it is necessary that he give full obedience to the instructions given him in order that he may not fail in the Work, and thus be delayed.

THE AETH MYSTERY

THOUGHT MAGIC

Because there have been men in times past and in the present who could make use of these forces, and who could bring about results that seemed miraculous, the term Magic has been applied. This term is a misnomer, because, in fact, there is no such thing as a magical act. Magic is simply the knowledge of Natural Laws, the development of the Soul Powers in man and the employment of these powers to work in harmony with Natural Laws. This it is which brings about these results.

Magic in its true sense is not a vulgar art. It is a threefold religion of the Soul. Magic is the religion of the Magi, including, as it does, Religion, Philosophy, and Science. It has therefore nothing to do with vulgar practices; in fact, with no practices whatsoever except with those Sacred Mantrams and Invocations which bring man nearer to God; and as he nears God ,so will his powers increase in proportion, because no man can travel Godward without increasing his powers and his capabilities to do good, to be a creator, as is his Father a Creator. Though Magic is therefore nothing more nor less than the full use of the trained and developed mental faculties, Using these for the good of mankind generally, whether to help a soul or to frustrate the evil designs of man.

REALIZATION

Anticipation is greater than Realization, we have been taught. This is really true in so far as the external world is concerned; but in the Inner World, the Soul World, this is not true. In the external world we imagine things, we desire this or that; but all of these things have to do with the mortal, the material existence. There is nothing perfect on this plane. Therefore, as the mind pictures ideal conditions and feelings it naturally follows that the realization is not so perfect as desired because the imperfect shows even in the ultimate results. But, on the Inner, the Soul, Plane, it is far different because on that plane of being all things are perfect, and when man looks forward to the realization of those things which concern the Soul and its powers, he is not disappointed, for the very good reason that as he travels the Path he also nears the goal of peace of soul, and thus he seeks the Love World instead of the sense world, and while all things may seem to be wrong, while the Master might lose his all, there is yet a great realization of peace and contentment, because the real being, the real existence, is not touched by these things.

Thus it is that realization is the ultimate of the Great Work, and where the heart is wholly true to the Great Art there can be no disappointment when realization comes, because then the Soul of man is blended with the Soul of God, and man has actually reached Godhood and is at peace, at Oneness, not only with God, but with all things that exist, and at that moment he ceases to judge others or the acts of others, realizing that they do nothing except what they think is best for them to do. Then he realizes why one great teacher taught:

"JUDGE NOT"

To judge is to be judged by the same judgment. This is the Great Law.

THE OPERATION

The Operation in the Great Art is at once difficult and not difficult. It is difficult for him who goes into it with some secret reservation in the heart, some lack of faith, some secret desire not belonging to the Art; but to him who enters the Work heart-whole and with a true desire it is not a labor, but a work of

THE AETH MYSTERY

love, and each step adds but a greater love for the Work and all things in general, and it is this increasing love which helps to build, to draw in, and to store, the great power possessed by the Master.

He who is most willing to give his all without question, to trust the Hierarchic Powers most fully, he it is who will reap the greatest benefits in the quickest time; and for this reason Jesus taught men: "Take no thought for the morrow," knowing full well that if the thought in the heart is pure and the trust is complete there can be no failure in realization.

It is also for this very reason that we see men who were rich and accustomed to the greatest luxuries in life gave their all without question to the Great Art. Though this seemed foolish and the direct means of suffering and self-denial, yet they reaped almost immediately just as much as they had given, though often in a different manner; and the fact remains that none of them ever regretted it, and they became the Masters of the ages, never to be forgotten. This we see not only in those who follow the Great Art, but we find it a fact in all the arts. Thus we find the artist who is an artist at heart. He enters his hovel, lives on bread and water, devotes his energies to his art and emerges a great and never-to-be-forgotten artist. This man might, if he wished, go out into the world and earn money in other ways, money enough to give him the luxuries; but his soul is not of that kind. Instead of that, he lives for his art, gives his whole body and soul to it, denies himself everything and the results- the Hierarchic Powers watch over him and he becomes the master of his art and his soul is happy and contented and at peace with God and man.

PRACTICAL DETAILS

In such teachings it is not theory that the Neophyte is to receive, but it is practical instructions and formulas such as he can readily follow, and it is just such instructions, just such training, that the Neophyte receives from the Aeth Fraternity. There are thousands of books that give theory, thousands of books that give an idea of the Great Art, give details of that which has been accomplished by the old Masters and Initiates. All these books, if written by Masters, are of great importance to the Neophyte because they are the foundation; but they are worthless as to practice, and it is in practice only where direct help, the direct teaching, of the guide and instructor is of benefit to the Neophyte.

For this one reason, if for no other, the Great Fraternity has never found it possible to teach the highest work to classes because every student is a distinct, separate individual, and, as no two are alike, it is impossible that that which meets the requirements of one will be able to meet the requirements of the other. For this reason each student must be taught separately and as an individual, and just as the student considers himself as such, applies the teachings to himself and considers no one else, nor the acts of any one else, will be able to succeed. Here again we must bring in the Great Law as taught by the Master Jesus, when he said: "JUDGE NOT."

We find that in many instances where there is failure on the part of the Neophyte it is directly traceable to the breaking of this command. Many Neophytes, instead of giving their whole attention to themselves and the Work, are prone to look beyond themselves, to watch the acts of other men and women, even of other students, and to see what these others are doing, trying to judge or to apply to themselves the actions and the experiences of another The minute this is done there is a breakage in the Work, and this results adversely to themselves, while in no way affecting the other.

No matter what other men may be doing, no matter what

they think, no matter even what a student in the same school may be doing, this is neither the concern, not even the thought, of the other student. Each student has only to do with himself and himself alone, and in no way is he concerned with the thoughts, habits, desires, or acts of any other living person.

When once the Neophyte has reached the Mastery, then it is that he can bring his powers into play and use them in helping others, provided such others desire and request his help. Or he may use his powers in the prevention of a wrong where he sees that it is clearly a thing that may hurt another, but even then the use of this power must be silent and solely because he desires only that good shall be done. Realization can come only to him who works toward that end, and until realization comes man must stand alone, be free from thoughts concerning others and even be free from caring for the insults, the condemnation, or the ignoring of others, which so often follow when the Neophyte enters the path.

ARCANUM LODGE

There are two distinct Churches, Lodges, or Temples-One of these is the external place of meeting, where members of a church or organization assemble together. But there is another, a greater meeting place, and this is within the individual The Master, the Initiate, becomes a Lodge, or Temple, within himself, complete in every appointment, and when he attends the Temple meeting it is within his inner self, and those present are none other than the Hierarchies.

The Aeth Fraternity has an outer meeting place or Temple. But the first and mo,st important work is for the Neophyte to develop himself and the Soul within himself so that he becomes a perfect universe, complete in all his appointments, and then he is more ready for the external organization where he

THE AETH MYSTERY

can meet others who think and do as he does. Of the external organization it is not our desire to speak here. Sufficient to say that, as time goes on, as Neophytes enter the Fraternity and reach toward the summit of Initiation, it is proposed not only to confer the Exalted Degrees in their external form, but once again to build such Temples and have such sublime worship as had the ancient Egyptian Priest-Initiates.

THE IMPERIAL DEGREE

This is not an outer or ceremonial degree, but refers to the highest phase of development in which the Neophyte can engage, and rapidly approaches the state of Initiation, enabling the student to reach that stage of Illumination which will make of him an Initiate-Priest, and thus enable him to help in the Great Work. This has well been called the Deific Degree, or the Degree of the Great Breath, because in reality it is such. Thus it is that "by coming into touch with this Deific Degree of the Great Breath the man becomes a creator in the real sense, and it lies in his power to create and establish real changes and tangible, material things in this life and world." So taught one of the Masters, so have held the other Masters for the past many centuries.

CREATIVE INVOCATIONS

In this booklet, which is for the general seeker, it is neither possible nor allowable to say much concerning this part of the Great Art. Sufficient is it to say that if the Neophyte has passed the other stages of the training he is then taught the Sacred Invocative Work, which will give him the real instruments for the accomplishment of the Great Art. These are not new, but are those of the most ancient Initiates. Though given in new words, to meet modern requirements, they are like the ancient work, as taught in the most ancient Temple,s, and no one will deny that it was then when the Holy Art was in its highest stage of development.

THE MASTER MYSTERY

The student is taught: "It is the Great Breath which is the Matrix from which are created all things existing. It is the Lesser Breath from which the physical being is being daily created. And it is from this same Matrix, or Lesser Breath, that it is possible for you to create all things reasonable this world which you desire."

In these Imperial Mysteries the Neophyte is taught all the things that the Ancient Initiate taught, and which gave them such power. The Neophyte who is obedient, who practices the Work, must of necessity come to know the power that is conferred on one so living, so practicing. It is to be borne in mind that neither the Fraternity nor any of its men make any claims whatsoever. They simply give, teach, state, that which the Ancient Fraternity claimed to be a fact, and which they proved to be a fact by the works that they accomplished.

If in a booklet of this nature, we were to claim all that the secret lessons themselves contain and make possible we would at once be considered as stating many things that are untruths. We therefore do nothing of the kind, but simply indicate that which was claimed by the Fraternity in the past, stating facts as they are, claiming nothing for ourselves or what we may be able to do. At the same time we frankly state that we cannot give a tenth part of that which is claimed for the Sacred Art.

One of our Initiates once said that it would be well to read the books written by Van der Naillen in order to get an idea of the powers possessed by the Initiate, and that of these books

THE AETH MYSTERY

the best one is 'On the Heights of Himalay.' We believe that this is true, because then the seeker, the would-be Neophyte, would get an idea a,s to what one may do who is willing to learn, to know, to dare, and to keep silent.

The lessons in their highest form, as given by the Aeth Fraternity, are such as will develop these powers in those who will practice and live the teachings.

INVOCATIONS

Not only i,s the first Invocation taught the Neophyte, but as he becomes master of the practice the Arch-Invocation of the Ancient Initiate is also taught him; and nothing short of failure to master the work can prevent him from being able to use these Invocations and reap results therefrom.

THE SACRED AUM INVOCATION

Besides the two former Invocations, the Aum Invocation of the true Initiates of old India is also taught, and it is safe to say that this Invocation is taught by no other Fraternity now in existence. For these reasons it is of such vast importance that this Fraternity, in one way or another, should be enabled to reach all those throughout the entire world who are truly interested and who desire the Highest and Most Sublime form of the Mystic and the Occult.

And it is the desire of the Fraternity to reach all such, it's desire to train them thoroughly, and, when ,so trained and found loyal to the Priesthood, then to have them teach the Lesser Work to mankind at large, teaching them the Divine Laws, which will help to bring peace on earth, good will to all men and establish such a Priesthood, such a School, that ignorance will give way to knowledge, and as knowledge takes the place of ignorance then will crime, sin, sickness, and suffering cease. This is the object and the aim of the Aeth Priesthood, nothing more, nothing less.

THE SPIRIT AND FIRE DEGREE, CALLED THE DEGREE OF CREATIVE LIFE

The ultimate of all Initiation is to find the source of Life. Every true philosopher of the pa,st, every true Initiate has made a claim that this is possible, and with some of the old philosophers this was the whole theme. That this is possible is now no longer doubted. That few have found it we know; that the many can find it we believe and claim to be true. But in order that this may be accomplished man must be fully prepared. Preparation is effected only through a training that considers the whole man.

Such a training the Aeth Priesthood gives its Neophytes, and when such training has been completed it is then that the Neophyte is given the instructions and the training that are covered by the Degree of Fire. Fire or heat is the underlying principle of all life. Where heat leaves there will we fail to find life Just as long as there is heat just that long does life remain. It is therefore the whole problem to keep this heart ever going. This idea was represented in the Ancient Temple by the Virgin Vestals' ever watching the Sacred Fire, never allowing it it burn out, under penalty of death.

Of what this work consists it is not even our desire to speak here. Sufficient is it to state that the work is fully and completely taught, and that even in the present age it has been proved that the work is founded on a sound basis because, through it, has been accomplished the Regeneration and the Rejuvenation of the whole man, from weakness to strength, from approaching death to new life.

THE AETH MYSTERY

CRITICISM

We may be criticized, in fact have been criticized, for taking this method of giving information concerning the Sacred Art and concerning the Aeth Fraternity, it being stated, apparently with justice, that the Ancient Fraternity look no such method of giving knowledge concerning its work.

Freely do we admit that they did not; but, on the contrary, they had a far more sensational method of allowing the people to learn of their work than have we. "And how?" will the sincere seeker ask. Easily answered. The ancient Fraternity had its Feast Days and its days of rejoicing. It was on these public holidays that the Priesthood, arrayed in its most costly and most beautiful regalia, would appear in parade before all the people, followed by its thousands of Neophytes and Devotees, and through that method draw from the masses its brightest and its richest youths, who would on entering give up title and wealth in order to become one of the Priest-Initiates. In our material age this is no longer possible. Institutions which were then the glory of the world are not now possible. Men are not willing to give up their all, their very life, in order that the Fraternity may reach the sublime heights it then did. Therefore it is not possible for the Fraternity of today to employ the methods used then. The Fraternity of today must satisfy itself with taking the best methods that present themselves in order that its sublime work and teachings may be known to those who are truly interested. It does not parade its work nor thrust its literature before those who have no desire either for religion or for philosophy or for the Sacred Arts.

ITEMS OF INFORMATION

A Scholarship in the Aeth Priesthood is for life. This

THE AETH MYSTERY

includes the necessary text-books, the lessons of instructions, the privileges of personal letters without limit, and the personal training.

OTHER BOOKS

It is not required of the student that he should buy other books, although if he so desires he is at liberty to do so. From time to time he will be informed of such books as would be a help to him, though, as already stated, these are not absolutely necessary.

LOYALTY

It is required of each and every student that he shall be loyal to the Order and its instructions. To show disloyalty, to speak ill of, or to do anything that might dishonor the Order, will cause the instructions and training to cease automatically. The Order cannot harbor traitors within its ranks.

THE NEOPHYTE'S DUTY

When the Neophyte enrolls with this School it is with the distinctive understanding that he shall obey such teachings and follow such instructions until he finds one of two things- either that the teachings are correct or that they are false. If he is sincere and faithful the instructions can not fail to bring about the desired results. The Fraternity cannot under any circumstances accept or tolerate any criticism or judgment from any of its Neophytes. Under the very nature of things, the one applying for instructions considers that he has need of them. This being granted, then it follows that, since the student is less than the teacher, the student should receive and obey and not take upon himself to attempt to criticize and to judge, or to instruct, wherein he is ignorant and in need of instruction.

THE AETH MYSTERY

The attitude of the Neophyte must in all cases be that of one who receives and is willing to obey. Moreover, it is an absolute rule of the Fraternity that students shall follow instructions and report. To do otherwise automatically stops the instructions and the training, because the Fraternity cannot allow a Neophyte to receive one lesson when the former one has not been mastered and reported upon.

IMPORTANT THINGS IN LIFE

In all important matters in life we find that those who desire to learn must, in the first place, be willing to obey. This we find not only in all branches of learning, but in all trades. This being true, it is but natural that the Mystic Fraternity, more than any other institution, must demand strict obedience and absolute loyalty to its institution and its instructors.

Moreover, the student should be willing to give this and to be faithful until he, like his teachers, has reached Initiation.

The vast number of Neophytes claim to be in advance of other members of the common humanity. And as advancement always means loyalty we should naturally look for loyalty and trueness of heart and greatness of soul; but in all ages it has been found that in many instances instead of loyalty and greatness of soul, there is a destructive egotism which sets itself up as judge, and in consequence the Neophyte thinks himself greater than the master or teacher, attempts to give instructions rather than accepting them and, like Lucifer, is cast out forever. Thus it has even been. Thus it must ever be. But the true Neophyte, he who is faithful, will ever be the one who will win, and who will be many times rewarded for his faithfulness just as men are rewarded in all walks of life for faithfulness and sincerity.

THE AETH MYSTERY

APPEALS FOR HELP

The Neophyte is at all times at liberty to appeal to the Brotherhood for such help as it can give, and this help will be given willingly, cheerfully, and without compensation. Gifts, donations, etc., will be accepted and will be used in spreading the work, especially its teachings of the Divine Laws, which are for mankind generally.

TEACHERS

It is the desire of the Fraternity that those who reach Initiation shall become healers and teachers. To those who show sufficient interest, the Lesser Work is to be taught to mankind generally.

OBLIGATION OF SILENCE

Although there is necessary an obligation of silence, this obligation in no way interferes with the duties of life, but has solely to do with the private books and lessons, teachings which are to be considered at all times sacred and secret, and not to be divulged to any one. As a necessary feature of growth, silence is enjoined upon the Neophyte in regard to experience, and phenomena attendant upon the Drills and practices of the Sacred Art- These he reports to his teacher alone.

THE PRIVATE BOOKS

On account of the nature of these books, it is fully understood that they are strictly private, for the use of the student only, given to him as between teacher and student, or physician and patient, that they are printed, but not published, and on no account are they for general use.

THE AETH MYSTERY

THE FEE

The fee paid at the time of enrollment is for a Life Scholarship, and the student will not be called upon to pay any additional fee.

It is to be clearly understood that this fee is not paid for knowledge nor for instructions, because knowledge can not be bought, but that it is paid only for the purpose of meeting legitimate expenses connected with the work and to help spread information concerning the Great Art and for the promulgation of the Lesser Teachings, called Soul Science, among the people generally.

ADDRESSING OF LETTERS

All letters and other matter must be addressed as indicated at end of this booklet. All monies must also be made payable in the same manner. No letter is to be addressed directly to the Fraternity. Letters so addressed will not be received.

THE GOVERNING POWER

The governing body of the Fraternity is composed of those who have thoroughly proven their worth, who have proven that they are willing to give their very life for the Sacred Work of the Fraternity. These who so rule have sworn not to be governed by the opinion of any one, not even by the most worthy of the members, but to rule only as instructed by the Hierarchic Powers.

This governing body and the men composing it are therefore unknown, except to those few who have the work in hand, and these few are under solemn oath not to betray any of them.

As plenipotentiaries or agents with full powers are appointed by the Hierarchic ruling body, these may become known to students and even to those outside of the Fraternity, but these must not be considered as of the governing body, but only as workers for the Great Order.

Even to these, when known, no letters must be addressed, directly, nor must money be made payable to them, but only to the special department of the Publishing Firm which oversees the publication of private text-books and such other printed matter as belongs to the Fraternity. All such communications and monies will at once be turned over to the proper parties and will have their immediate attention- Address only:

THE PHILOSOPHICAL PUBLISHING CO.,
Dept. C. ALLENTOWN, PA.

THE END

CPSIA information can be obtained
at www.ICGtesting.com
Printed in the USA
LVHW081344110419
613817LV00035B/701/P